*Double-handed
backhand drive*

*High-driven
forehand*

*Throwing the
ball up to serve*

Low-driven backhand

Practising ball control

THE YOUNG
TENNIS
PLAYER

ARANTXA
SANCHEZ VICARIO

Pressurized tennis balls

Take-back for a backhand smash

Ready position

Follow-through for a forehand drive

DK

London • New York • Stuttgart

Backhand drop shot

A DORLING KINDERSLEY BOOK

Editor Francesca Stich   **Art editor** Rebecca Johns

Project editor Fiona Robertson

Photography Matthew Ward

Picture research Sharon Southren

Production Charlotte Traill

Deputy editorial director Sophie Mitchell
Deputy art director Miranda Kennedy

The young tennis players
Nick Çava Day, Nick Hamnabard, Jessica London, Faye Mason,
Vishal Nayyar, Namita Shah, and Steven Vance

First published in Great Britain in 1996 by
Dorling Kindersley Limited
9 Henrietta Street, London WC2E 8PS

A CIP catalogue record for this book is available from the British Library.

ISBN 0 7513 5393 0

Colour reproduction by Colourscan, Singapore
Printed and bound in Italy by L.E.G.O.

Contents

To all young players

" TENNIS HAS ALWAYS BEEN part of my life. As the youngest in a family with four professional tennis players, I began to play tennis when I was four years old. I valued the time and advice that people gave me and began to spend every spare minute on a tennis court. I decided to make a career out of the game and turned professional ten years later, at the age of 14. When I was 17, I won my first Grand Slam title, the French Open. In 1994, I won the French Open again, as well as the US Open, and was ranked Number One in the world that year. If you are a tennis enthusiast, I know you'll enjoy reading this book. Tennis is a 'sport for all', and whatever your ability, this book will improve your understanding and increase your enjoyment of the game. "

Arantxa Sánchez Vicario

Left-handed players
Whenever you see this sign, the pictures show a left-handed player.

Buzzing with confidence
Determination is one of the most important skills a professional tennis player must learn. My opponents nicknamed me "the Bumblebee" because of my determined spirit and the speed with which I move around the court.

This is a cross court shot with topspin.

This shows the flight of a short, angled shot.

Talking tactics
As well as the amazing step-by-step photography throughout this book, you will see these diagrams. I have tried to give you tactical advice on each of your shots. Remember, however, that as your game improves, you will learn your own strengths and weaknesses and develop your favourite shots as well.

Olympic Games
When I was at the 1992 Olympic Games, Conchita Martinez and I won a silver medal in the doubles. I also earned myself a bronze medal in the women's singles. This was especially nice since the 1992 Olympics were held in my home country.

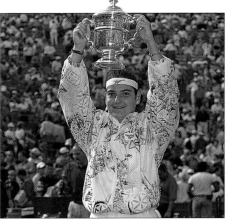

At the US Open
Here I am holding the trophy at the US Open. In 1994, I won both the singles and the doubles titles at the US Open. I am the first player to achieve both wins at once since Martina Navratilova in 1987.

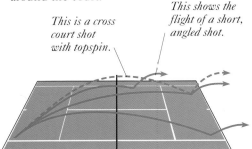

History of tennis

FROM THE GREEK wall paintings of Themistocles we know that an ancient form of tennis was played as far back as 500 BC. During the 15th century Real, or Royal, tennis was developed in France from a game called *Jeu de Paume* (game of the palm). Real tennis was originally played in monastery cloisters and is still occasionally played by enthusiasts. Lawn tennis, or tennis as we know it today, became popular during Queen Victoria's reign, when it was played on the lawns of stately homes. It was not until the early 1870s that tennis was played as a serious sport. The first tennis championships were held at the All England Croquet and Lawn Tennis Club at Wimbledon, London, in July 1877. Some 200 spectators watched the first men's final. More than 15,000 fill the centre court stands at Wimbledon now.

Young Americans
May Sutton of America was only 18 years old when she won her first Wimbledon title in 1905. Here, you can see just how much tennis equipment and clothing have changed over the last century.

Skirt sensation
In the 1920s, tennis became very popular. Suzanne Lenglen of France, seen here winning the women's singles at Wimbledon in 1922, was the first woman to wear a shorter dress and short sleeves. Lenglen was also one of the first players to turn professional.

International team tennis
The first international team competition was the Davis Cup in 1900. During the 1920s, Bill Tilden of America never lost a singles match in the Davis Cup challenge rounds. For many years only Britain, France, Australia, and America took part. Today, more than 100 countries participate in the Davis Cup.

19th century tennis set
Most early racket frames were made from one solid piece of ash wood like the one above. Today they are made from carbon graphite or fibreglass. Rackets can still be any weight or shape but must measure less than 81.28 cm (32 in) in length and 31.75 cm (12.5 in) across.

Tennis today
For professional players, tennis is a way of life. Some professionals will travel the world 20 times in their career. There are dozens of tournaments every year and I have even represented my country at the Olympics. I miss my home in Andorra, but playing tennis is very satisfying and the rewards compensate for the time I dedicate to the game.

Sporting hero
Powerful Bjorn Borg of Sweden won the Wimbledon men's singles for five years running (from 1976 to 1980). Only two other men have achieved this.

Getting started

ANYONE CAN START to play tennis. All you need is a borrowed tennis racket, an old tennis ball, and a wall to hit against. If you enjoy this, then invite a friend to play on a court at your local park. To become more experienced, you may want to join a tennis club that has a good junior coaching programme. As you start to play more regularly, your game will improve. At this stage you might like to get some of your own equipment. The two most important items are a suitable racket and proper tennis shoes.

Boys' clothes
Tennis clothes should be loose-fitting and made from natural, lightweight materials. In order to keep within the standard rules of most tennis clubs, you should wear mainly white shorts, socks, and a shirt. Sometimes you can wear patterned shirts or partially coloured clothes. To begin with, your school sports kit will probably be fine.

Tennis shoes
Comfortable, well-made tennis shoes are extremely important. Cushioning in the sole will reduce the amount of vibration in your ankles and legs when you are running. They should also support your instep and the tendons at the back of your heel. Buy shoes that are suitable for indoor and outdoor court surfaces.

A leather upper will be more hard-wearing than canvas.

Reinforced toe cap protects the shoe and your toes.

Perforations in the shoe allow air to circulate and keep your feet cool.

Towelling socks absorb sweat and give extra cushioning.

A lightweight but sturdy rubber sole is designed to provide maximum grip.

If you have long hair, keep it tied back away from your face.

Polo shirts are traditional and popular tennis wear.

Shorts should have pockets to keep a spare ball.

Shoe size
Make sure you buy shoes that are the right size or you may get blisters.

A thermal racket carrier protects your rackets when you're not using them. The shoulder strap makes it easy to carry and there is also a compartment for balls.

Girls' clothes
The same mainly white clothing rule applies to girls as well as boys. Most girls wear either a tennis dress or a skirt with a shirt, but you can wear a pair of shorts if you prefer. Do not wear jewellery as it can catch in your clothing.

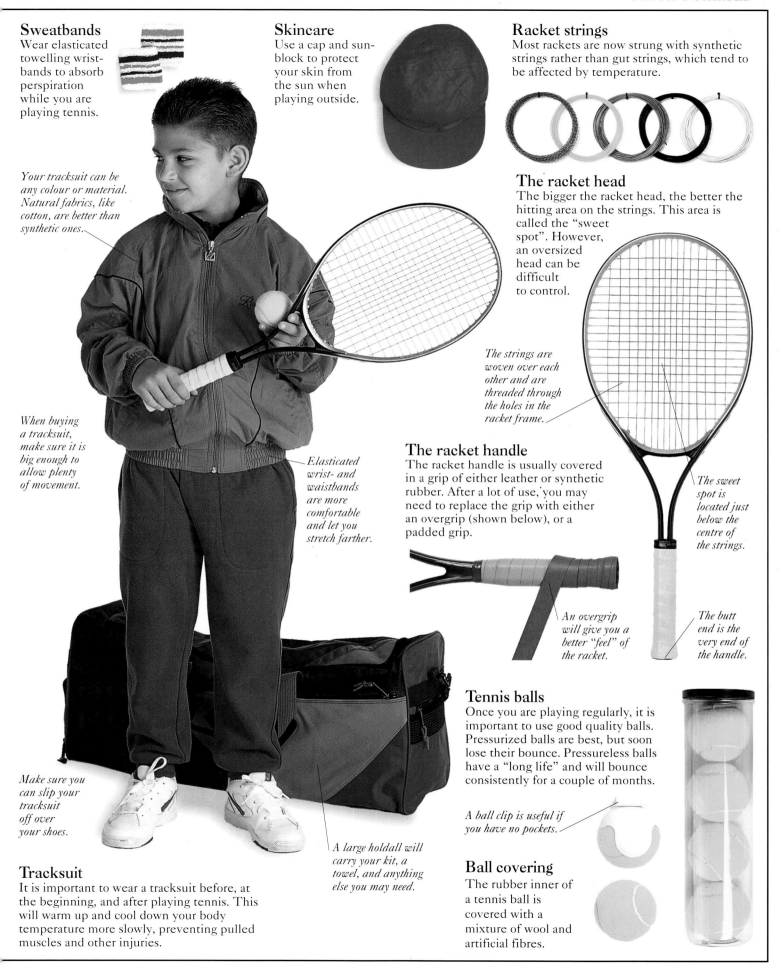

Sweatbands
Wear elasticated towelling wristbands to absorb perspiration while you are playing tennis.

Skincare
Use a cap and sunblock to protect your skin from the sun when playing outside.

Racket strings
Most rackets are now strung with synthetic strings rather than gut strings, which tend to be affected by temperature.

Your tracksuit can be any colour or material. Natural fabrics, like cotton, are better than synthetic ones.

The racket head
The bigger the racket head, the better the hitting area on the strings. This area is called the "sweet spot". However, an oversized head can be difficult to control.

When buying a tracksuit, make sure it is big enough to allow plenty of movement.

The strings are woven over each other and are threaded through the holes in the racket frame.

The racket handle
The racket handle is usually covered in a grip of either leather or synthetic rubber. After a lot of use, you may need to replace the grip with either an overgrip (shown below), or a padded grip.

Elasticated wrist- and waistbands are more comfortable and let you stretch farther.

The sweet spot is located just below the centre of the strings.

An overgrip will give you a better "feel" of the racket.

The butt end is the very end of the handle.

Make sure you can slip your tracksuit off over your shoes.

Tennis balls
Once you are playing regularly, it is important to use good quality balls. Pressurized balls are best, but soon lose their bounce. Pressureless balls have a "long life" and will bounce consistently for a couple of months.

A ball clip is useful if you have no pockets.

A large holdall will carry your kit, a towel, and anything else you may need.

Tracksuit
It is important to wear a tracksuit before, at the beginning, and after playing tennis. This will warm up and cool down your body temperature more slowly, preventing pulled muscles and other injuries.

Ball covering
The rubber inner of a tennis ball is covered with a mixture of wool and artificial fibres.

The court and game

WHEN YOU STEP OUT on court to play a match, you will need to understand some basic rules of tennis. Try to learn what all the court markings are for as these are the boundaries that limit your drives, volleys, and serves. Know when and where to return the ball and how to score. Observe the unwritten rules about behaviour and etiquette. This means that you must be fair and honest at all times, especially when calling the score after every point. Finally, decide who will serve first by tossing a coin or spinning a racket. Most importantly, get out there and play!

Court surfaces

Tennis can be played on a variety of court surfaces, each of which affect the bounce of the ball in a different way. A slow court is one with a rough surface, such as clay. This makes the ball bounce higher and more slowly. A fast court surface, such as grass, is one that causes the ball to skid quickly as it bounces.

Singles sideline 11.89 m (39 ft) long

Baseline centre mark or small T

Short tennis

If you find full-sized tennis difficult at first, you could learn to play short tennis. This will help you to develop your tennis strokes and teach you how to move and position yourself on court. Short tennis is played using lightweight rackets and sponge balls. It is played on a badminton court which is considerably smaller than a full-sized tennis court, with a baseline of only 6.1 m (20 ft) and sideline of 13.4 m (44 ft). There are only 11 points in a game, but the game must be won by two clear points after the score reaches 10-10. Once you have mastered short tennis, you can move on to play transition tennis (see opposite page).

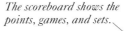

For short tennis, the badminton net is lowered to 78 cm (2 ft 7 in).

The short tennis court has no tramlines or service boxes.

Tennis scoring system

Game Starting at 0, or "love", one player must win four points called 15, 30, 40, and game.

Deuce If the score is deuce (40-40), the game continues until one player wins by two clear points: the advantage point, then the game point. If you lose the advantage point the score returns to deuce.

Set The first player to win six games wins the set, but the winner must be at least two clear games in front. If the score in a set reaches 5-5, play seven games. If it is 6-6, play the first to seven points (a tiebreak) and whichever player wins the tiebreak, wins the game and set.

Match A match is usually the best of three sets (five sets in men's professional matches).

The scoreboard shows the points, games, and sets.

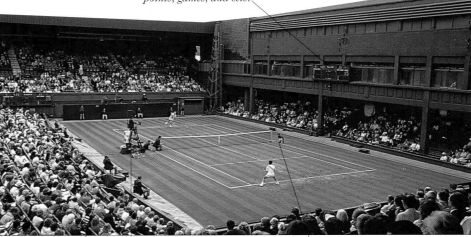

The linesmen and lineswomen are positioned around the court to call faults.

The umpire has a good view of the court from a high chair next to the net. The umpire's decision is final and he or she announces the score after every point.

The ball boys and girls pick up every loose ball.

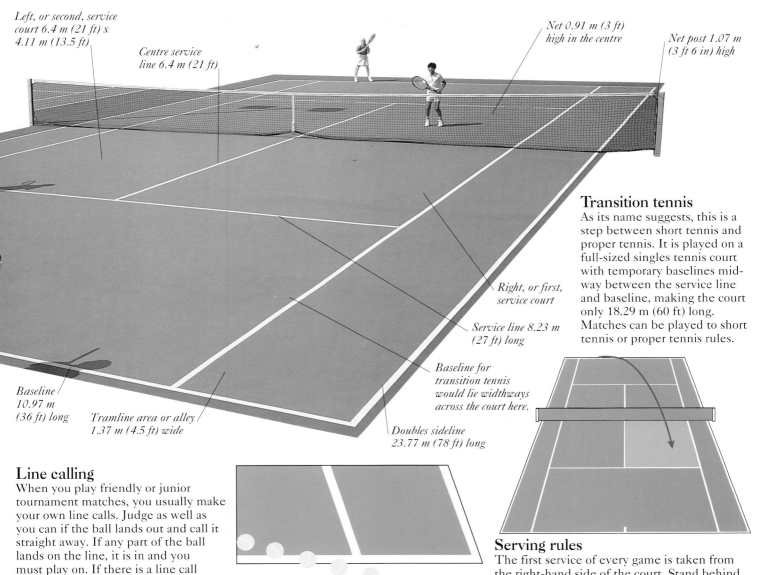

Left, or second, service court 6.4 m (21 ft) x 4.11 m (13.5 ft)

Centre service line 6.4 m (21 ft)

Net 0.91 m (3 ft) high in the centre

Net post 1.07 m (3 ft 6 in) high

Right, or first, service court

Service line 8.23 m (27 ft) long

Baseline for transition tennis would lie widthways across the court here.

Baseline 10.97 m (36 ft) long

Tramline area or alley 1.37 m (4.5 ft) wide

Doubles sideline 23.77 m (78 ft) long

Transition tennis

As its name suggests, this is a step between short tennis and proper tennis. It is played on a full-sized singles tennis court with temporary baselines mid-way between the service line and baseline, making the court only 18.29 m (60 ft) long. Matches can be played to short tennis or proper tennis rules.

Line calling

When you play friendly or junior tournament matches, you usually make your own line calls. Judge as well as you can if the ball lands out and call it straight away. If any part of the ball lands on the line, it is in and you must play on. If there is a line call disagreement, then play the point again. This is called a let (a second chance).

Only this ball is out as all the others are touching the line.

Positive thinking

When I am on court I try to concentrate completely on my game and put such determination into every shot in order to win. If I lose a point I try to put it out of my mind immediately. Thinking too much about mistakes can cause you to play the next point badly. Keep calm, take each point one at a time and play as well as you can. All professionals learn to think like this, and if you want to do well, so should you.

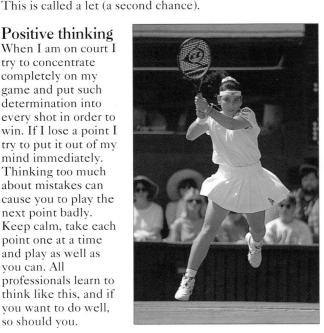

Serving rules

The first service of every game is taken from the right-hand side of the court. Stand behind the baseline and serve diagonally so that the ball bounces into your opponent's service box. Alternate from right to left courts to serve for each new point. Each player serves for a full game, swapping ends after every other game. If the serve hits the top of the net and lands in, then a let is called, and the serve is taken again.

Court etiquette

Tennis is a very competitive sport and sometimes players find it difficult to control their behaviour on court. Never argue over a line call, settle for a let if you disagree with your opponent and take the point again. Although it is important to be friendly, don't let your opponent walk all over you. Try to be fair and play your best game. Whether you win or lose, thank your opponent for playing.

Preparing to play

BEFORE YOU START playing tennis, you should go through a stretching and movement routine to warm up. Warming up will loosen your muscles and joints, making you more flexible. This will make your heart beat faster and can help to prevent injury. It will prepare you to move more quickly and stretch farther on court. Going through an exercise routine before a match can also help you to concentrate. Practise additional exercises at the side of the court to test your reactions and speed as footwork and timing are essential skills!

Groin stretch
This exercise will stretch your inner leg and groin area. Sit on the ground, bring the soles of your shoes together, and pull your ankles towards your body. To increase the stretch try pushing down slowly and gently on your knees with your elbows. Hold the position for 20 seconds, then relax. Repeat three times.

Keep your back straight.

Keep your ankles on the floor.

Leg stretch
This exercise stretches the hamstrings at the back of your legs. Sit on the ground with your legs outstretched in front of you. With the backs of your knees on the floor, reach for your toes. If you cannot touch your toes, then reach as far as you can. Hold the position for 20 seconds, then relax. Repeat three times.

Keep your feet together and the backs of your knees against the floor.

Shoulder stretch
Warm up your upper arm and shoulder area with this exercise. Stand upright and use one arm to try to touch the bottom of your shoulder blade. Use the other hand to pull back gently on the elbow of your bent arm. Keep your head up and hold the position for 20 seconds. Repeat three times with each arm.

Keep your back straight throughout this exercise.

Face forwards while moving.

Figure-of-eight
Improve your footwork and agility with this exercise. Place two tennis balls on the floor 1 m (3 ft) apart. Move as quickly as you can in a figure-of-eight pattern around the balls. Take small steps and stay low to help you keep your balance. Count how many times you can complete the figure-of-eight in a minute, then change direction and do the same exercise the other way.

Move smoothly
When stretching it is important never to bounce or jerk the movement.

Use your hands for balance.

Keep your knees bent.

Keeping your steps small, run as close to the tennis balls as you can.

Try not to lean forwards.

Side stretch
To stretch your waist and stomach muscles, stand upright with your feet shoulder-width apart. Place your right hand on your hip and lean to your right, keeping your feet on the floor. Bring your left arm over to increase the stretch. Hold for 20 seconds then do the same exercise on your left side. Repeat three times.

Quick reactions

To develop fast reactions you need to do exercises that test the speed at which you can move to the ball. Try the following game with a friend. Take it in turns to catch the ball.

1 Your partner holds the ball out in front of their body, while you rest your hand lightly on top of their hand.

Make sure the ball is facing the ground.

Stay on your toes.

2 At any time, your partner can drop the ball. You have to try to catch the ball before it bounces. If you find this difficult at first, ask your partner to hold the ball up higher.

Bring your hand under the ball as it drops.

Keep your feet apart to help you balance.

Watch the ball closely.

Both balls should be in the air at the same time.

Basic ball sense

Develop your hand-eye co-ordination with a partner by standing about 2 m (6 ft) apart and throwing each other a ball at the same time. Aim the ball carefully and throw underarm. To make it more difficult, clap or turn around before catching the ball.

Keep your knees bent.

Keep your feet shoulder-width apart for balance.

Ball control

To help your hitting co-ordination, bounce a ball up off your racket strings. Count how many times in a row you can hit the ball. To make it more difficult, try the same exercise without moving your feet. Hit the ball higher if you need more time.

Try to keep the racket between shoulder and knee height.

Cross-over steps

In tennis, it is important to move quickly and with good footwork, while keeping your balance at all times. To test your footwork and co-ordination, practise side-stepping along the baseline. Continue until you reach the end of the line, then do the opposite to travel back. Repeat three times.

1 From a standing position, travel to your left by bringing your right leg over and in front of your left leg.

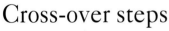 **Leg tension**
Try to bend your knees when you cross your legs, and straighten them when you side-step.

2 Bring your left leg across and into a wide side-step.

Always face forwards and keep your head still while you are moving.

3 Bring your right leg across and behind your left leg. Take another wide side-step with your left leg.

Use your hands for balance.

Stay on your toes.

Try to step lightly.

Handling the racket

WHEN YOU START PLAYING tennis, it is important that you learn how to handle your racket properly. Try to choose a racket that is suitable for your age and size; it should feel like a natural extension of your arm and hand. Junior rackets come pre-strung and measure from 52 to 64 cm (21 to 26 in) in length. They also vary in frame thickness, or width, from narrow- to wide-bodied and tend to be very light. When you hold the handle, there should be a small gap between the top of your little finger and the heel of your hand. The more comfortable the racket feels, the better you will hit the ball. The action of hitting the ball is called a stroke, and has three main stages: the preparation or take-back, the hit, and the follow-through.

Lightweight wide-bodied junior racket
Wide-bodied rackets are currently the lightest and most powerful type of racket. The broad side-on width makes them stronger than slimmer models.

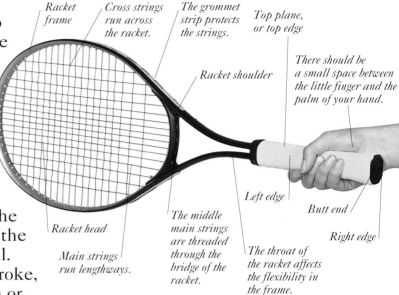

Racket frame

Cross strings run across the racket.

The grommet strip protects the strings.

Top plane, or top edge

Racket shoulder

There should be a small space between the little finger and the palm of your hand.

Left edge

Butt end

Right edge

Racket head

The middle main strings are threaded through the bridge of the racket.

The throat of the racket affects the flexibility in the frame.

Main strings run lengthways.

Forehand grips
The way a stroke feels when you hit the ball and the effect that the stroke has on the ball, largely depend on how you are holding the racket. This is called your racket grip. There are three main forehand grips: eastern, continental, and western. Each grip can be changed slightly for comfort. Hold the racket with your hand towards the butt end of the handle. This will give you room to add your other hand for double-handed grips. All grips are the same for left-handed players. Follow these instructions using your left hand, remembering that the right edge of the racket becomes the left edge, and vice versa.

Eastern forehand grip
This is a very natural grip used to hit the ball at any height flat, or with topspin or slice. Simply shake hands with the racket. The "V" between your finger and thumb should be on the right edge of the racket handle. Spread your first finger up the racket handle for more support.

Keep the heel of your hand at the butt end of the racket. Place your palm behind the handle for extra support.

Continental grip
Use this grip to tackle low balls. Place the "V" made by your thumb and first finger so that it is slightly to the left of centre on the top plane of the handle. You may find it difficult to hit topspin with this grip.

Note the "V" between first finger and thumb.

Western forehand grip
This grip was developed in California, where cement courts make the ball bounce higher. Use a western forehand grip for heavy topspin, and to hit high-bouncing balls. Move the "V" towards the right edge of the handle. Place the knuckle of your first finger so that it is underneath the handle and wrap your thumb around the top.

Your wrist will be naturally bent backwards by this grip.

Semi-western forehand grip
This grip is a modified western grip, in which your wrist position is less exaggerated. Use this grip for extra topspin and to hit high-bouncing balls. The "V" between your finger and thumb should sit on the right edge of the handle. The knuckle of your first finger should be on the lower right edge and your thumb should wrap around the handle.

It is difficult to hit low, wide balls using semi-western forehand grip.

Backhand grips

There are two ways of holding the racket for a backhand stroke: single-handed or double-handed. Most players use a double-handed grip for extra support and power on their backhand. This also avoids making a grip change after playing a forehand shot. If you do find that you prefer to use one hand, always try to change your grip so you don't bend your wrist awkwardly when adding topspin to a stroke. If you are playing a sliced backhand, try to use a continental or an eastern backhand grip.

Eastern backhand grip

Eastern backhand is used for topspin and slice. Place the "V" on the left edge of the handle and the knuckle of your first finger on the upper left edge of the racket. Wrap your thumb around the handle.

Spread your first finger slightly up the handle for extra strength and flexibility.

Strong eastern backhand grip

Use this grip for heavy topspin. Place the knuckle of your first finger on the top plane of the handle, and the "V" at the bottom left. If you use a strong eastern backhand grip, be aware that you need time for a greater change of grip (see page 21) between strokes.

Double-handed grip without change

This can only be done if you use an eastern grip for your forehand drive. With your playing hand in an eastern forehand grip at the butt end of the handle, simply add the other hand, also using eastern forehand. Be aware that a double-handed grip limits your reach for wide balls, and in those cases it is best to play a single-handed shot. If you usually play with a western or semi-western forehand grip, then you will need to change your grip for a double-handed backhand.

Double-handed grip with change

This grip change is especially useful for hitting heavy topspin on your backhand and can be effective when receiving a high-bouncing ball. With your playing hand in either an eastern backhand or strong eastern backhand grip, place your other hand higher on the handle in an eastern forehand or semi-western forehand grip.

Mirror image
Try holding a mirror alongside these pictures to see the left-handed positions on the handle.

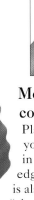

Modified continental grip

Place the "V" between your finger and thumb in the centre of the top edge of the handle. This is also known as the "chopper" grip, because if you imagine you are chopping wood with the racket edge, your hand will naturally grip the handle correctly. This grip is ideal for volleying because you won't have time to change your grip between backhand and forehand volleys. It is also the best grip for serving as it allows for plenty of wrist action. However, you will need to have a strong wrist.

Hold your racket up and watch the ball.

Bent knees will help you spring into action.

Ready position

Once you have mastered how to hold your racket, you are ready to start playing. One of the most basic positions in tennis is the ready position. It is used to receive the service and as a "home base" position between shots. Your ready position should be relaxed and focused, with knees bent and toes prepared to push off the ground, in reaction to your opponent's shot. Keep your racket central so that you can prepare it quickly on either side.

The five fundamental skills

There are five basic skills which players of all ages and levels should try to develop in order to produce strokes of a high standard.
1. Do not take your eyes off the ball.
2. Speedy footwork to the ball and quick recovery for the next shot.
3. Good balance, keeping a low centre of gravity and a still head.
4. Control of the racket swing, throw, or punch.
5. Awareness of the height and angle of the racket face at the point of contact with the ball.

Forehand drive

THERE ARE TWO TYPES of groundstroke: forehand drive and backhand drive. Groundstrokes are played after the ball has bounced once. For most players, the forehand drive is their strongest stroke and is usually the one that they learn first. Try to develop this stroke so that you can rely on it for rallying and attacking. Aim for a relaxed and well-timed swinging action which feels natural, not forced.

Positioning your feet
If you are right-handed, step forwards with your left foot (shown as violet); if you are left-handed, step with your right foot. This is called your front foot, and you use it to position yourself sideways-on to the ball. If you use a more open stance, step behind with your front foot (shown as blue).

Your forehand
Concentrate on each stage of your stroke: the take-back, hit, and follow-through. Remember the five basic skills (see page 17) to produce a smooth, controlled action.

Turn your shoulders as you bring your racket back.

Cocked wrist
Keep your wrist cocked back and lead with the butt end of the racket as you start to swing forwards.

Try using an eastern forehand grip.

1 Stand in the ready position, with your knees bent. Watch the ball and prepare your forehand grip as you move to make your shot.

2 In a low, compact position, start to take your racket back early, guiding it with your free hand to help turn your shoulders.

3 Take your racket back above shoulder height, so it forms a natural loop as it comes through for the hit.

Keep your knees bent.

Open stance forehand drive
When reaching for a wide forehand, many players like to hit the ball in less of a side-on position. This stance is useful for hitting a high-bouncing ball with a western or semi-western grip, but it is difficult to use for low shots. Open stance also helps to disguise the direction of your shot. Step forwards slightly with your front foot, but keep the weight on your back foot. As you swing through with your racket, push with your back leg so you "throw" your weight forwards into the ball.

Turn your shoulders and take your racket back fully.

Step forwards with your front foot.

Push with your back leg.

Quickly rotate your shoulders for extra power.

Step forwards with your front foot.

18

Topspin

Hitting a ball with topspin causes the ball to kick up after it bounces. A forehand drive with topspin can make the ball rise high over the net and deep into your opponent's court. Take the racket back as normal, but this time drop it into a deep loop so it is below the height of the approaching ball. Swing the racket upwards, brushing up behind the back of the ball and follow through over the other shoulder.

Mastering topspin

Use the top edge of the racket to brush upwards behind the back of the ball. The faster the racket moves, the more spin it will generate.

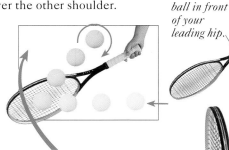

Turn your shoulders
Point towards the ball with your free hand. This keeps your shoulders turned and will help with your balance.

Keep the racket head low and aim to hit the ball in front of your leading hip.

Bend your knees.

Turn your shoulders quickly to hit the ball harder.

Talking tactics

A forehand groundstroke can be played from anywhere on court. Aim your shots deep down the line or diagonally across the court. Draw your opponent wide occasionally with short, angled shots.

Topspin shot aimed deep cross court.

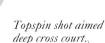

Keep your head still throughout the stroke.

5 Keep rotating your shoulders as you swing the racket through the hitting area (the area where you make your stroke).

Point your elbow in the direction of the ball.

Rotate your free arm along with your shoulders.

As you hit through the ball, straighten up with your front leg.

Your racket should meet the ball in front of your body.

6 With your body facing forwards, follow through with the racket over your other shoulder. Move your back foot forwards to keep your balance. This will also help you to recover for the next shot.

4 Drop the racket head a little and then drive it up into the ball to give the shot some lift. Rotate your shoulders and hit the ball between knee and shoulder height in front of your body.

Keep your weight on your front foot.

Bend your back leg as you bring it forwards so you can push off and recover quickly.

Ready position
After you have made your stroke, move back to a ready position behind the small T on the baseline.

Backhand drive

MOST PLAYERS BEGIN by using two hands on their backhand drive. You can progress to a single-handed stroke when you feel more confident, or continue to use two hands to give your stroke extra strength. Like the forehand drive, the backhand drive is a swinging action and you can use it to hit a ball flat, with topspin, or with slice. The backhand drive is often a harder stroke to master than the forehand, but with practice, you can develop it into a very powerful shot.

Positioning your feet
If you are right-handed, step forwards with your right foot as you hit your backhand drive (shown as violet). If you are left-handed, your left foot is your front foot. As with a forehand drive, you can also hit a backhand with an open stance (shown as blue).

Use either of the double-handed grips (see page 17).

1 Stand in the ready position. Watch the ball come off your opponent's racket so that you can respond as quickly as possible to their shot.

Keep your eyes focused on the ball.

2 Turn your shoulders and bring your racket straight back with your wrists cocked. Support your weight on your back foot.

Keep the racket head just above wrist height.

Double-handed backhand
Using two hands on your backhand will make you feel more confident. A double-handed backhand can also make your shot more powerful and will give you better control of both the racket and the ball.

Your feet should be shoulder-width apart.

3 Step into the ball as it comes towards you. Keep your knees bent and your shoulders turned.

Sliced backhand
A sliced ball will skid and bounce lower than normal. Try using a single-handed backhand to slice, even if you usually use two hands. This will allow you to reach farther for wide balls. Turn your shoulders and take the racket back high. Swing from high to low, hitting the ball slightly more to the side of your body than you would with a flat driven shot. Follow through sideways-on, and keep your racket head high.

Use a modified continental or eastern grip and support the racket head with your free hand.

Slicing the ball
Cutting from high to low behind the ball with your racket makes the ball float low over the net.

Lead with the bottom edge of the racket, keeping the racket head slightly open.

Follow through with your racket face open.

Single-handed backhand

This stroke allows you to reach farther for wide balls than you could with a double-handed backhand. A single-handed backhand can, with practice, be as powerful as a double-handed backhand. Take the racket back by turning your shoulders. Keep sideways-on as you swing through and hit the ball, then follow through with the racket high.

Point your front shoulder towards the ball.

Hit the ball in front of your body.

Keep your shoulder back for a bridged follow-through.

Keep your racket arm straight and support the racket head with your free hand.

Bend your knees as you step towards the ball.

Grip change

As you take the racket back on a single-handed backhand, use your free hand to turn the racket. Hold the throat of the racket with your free hand and change your grip to eastern backhand (see page 17).

Arched follow-through

To generate more topspin or to hit a high-bouncing ball, use an arched follow-through. Let the racket travel from low to high in an arch in front of your body. Contrary to the bridged follow-through above, let your other shoulder come around. Your racket will brush up behind the back of the ball.

Keep your wrists cocked to help control the flight of the ball.

Keep your head still.

Launch your body into the ball.

5 Still rotating your shoulders, swing the racket head out through the hitting area.

Stretch your arms so the contact point with the ball is in front of your body.

Point your elbow in the direction you want the ball to travel.

Shoulders are fully rotated and facing forwards.

Push forwards with your back foot.

4 Rotate your shoulders quickly and thrust your weight forwards.

Bring this foot around to help you recover for the next shot.

Talking tactics

A backhand drive can be played from anywhere on the court, depending on where the ball lands. Keep your shots deep down the line or cross court. Try to make your opponent run wide with short, angled shots.

Down-the-line topspin shot

6 Follow through over your other shoulder with both hands still holding your racket. Bring your back foot forwards for balance and to help you recover quickly.

The service

IN A TENNIS MATCH, the service, or serve, is the most important stroke. It is the first shot of every point, and if played well can give you an immediate advantage over your opponent. It is vital to develop a serve which you can repeat exactly over and over again. Try to make your service as difficult as possible for your opponent to return. Decide on the direction and length of each service before you begin and concentrate on accuracy rather than power. If you make a mistake, called a fault, you are allowed a second serve.

Throwing the ball
Practise your ball toss by standing in your serving position with your racket by your front foot. Toss the ball up in front of your body, slightly over to your racket side, and aim to bounce the ball off the racket face.

Holding the ball
Hold the ball lightly in your fingers. Have another ball in your pocket or ball clip ready for a second serve.

Preparing to serve

The serving action is a fluent movement which should feel as if you are "throwing" your racket at the ball. Try counting "one, two, three, and hit" to help your timing. "One" as you prepare your racket, "two" as your arms pass down by your legs, "three" as your racket goes back and you toss the ball up, "and hit" as you bring your racket through behind your head and hit the ball.

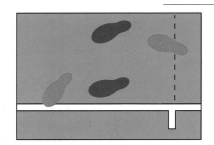

Positioning your feet
A foot fault (shown as red) is declared if you touch the baseline, step on the extension of the centre mark, or step on the sideline with either foot before hitting the ball. If you fault on your second service (a double fault), then you lose the point.

1 Stand behind the baseline with your body sideways-on to the court. Try to hold the racket with a modified continental grip (see page 17), as this will make it easier to put spin on the ball.

Keep both arms straight.

Rest the ball against the racket strings.

Before you serve
Wait until your opponent is in the ready position.

Feet shoulder-width apart

Make sure that your front foot is behind the baseline.

Place your weight on your back foot.

2 Bring both arms down slowly so that the ball hand touches your front leg and your racket hand brushes past your back leg.

Let the racket drop naturally.

Keep your racket shoulder back.

Bend your elbow.

3 Keep your racket arm away from the side of your body as you take your racket back. Your ball arm should be straight as you extend it above your head. Release the ball when your arm is fully stretched.

Begin to transfer your weight onto your front foot.

Topspin service

Using topspin will arch the ball over the net and make it kick up after the bounce. Throw the ball up towards your non-racket side. Turn your racket shoulder well back as you release the ball. As the ball starts to fall, spring up using your legs and bring your racket up almost edge-on to the ball. Take your racket up behind the back of the ball to create the topspin.

Slice service

This spin will make the ball curve sideways. Throw the ball up farther over to your racket side. Use a modified continental grip to bring the bottom edge of your racket around the ball. If you are right-handed, slice your racket from right to left around the back of the ball. If you are left-handed, slice your racket from left to right. Follow through across your body as usual.

Open stance service

When serving, it is not always necessary to bring your back foot forwards before hitting the ball. Pete Sampras of America, above, keeps his back foot behind because he feels more balanced in this position.

 Aim for accuracy
Do not try to make every first serve an ace. If you try to serve too hard, you will make mistakes.

Talking tactics

When playing singles, serve from near the centre-mark. Either hit diagonally into the service box down the centre of the court, into your opponent's body, or wide.

Wide topspin serve

4 Bend your racket arm, ready to hit the ball. Point with your ball arm to keep your back shoulder lower than your front.

Imagine you are throwing overarm with your racket arm.

Throw the ball slightly higher than you can reach with your racket.

Push your front hip into the court.

5 Rotate your shoulders until they are parallel with the net. Straighten your legs and reach up to hit the ball just as it begins to fall.

6 Feel the speed of the racket head overtake your wrist after you have hit the ball. Use your ball arm to keep your balance as your body twists.

Bend your knees.

Push up from your knees.

Bring your ball arm down.

7 On the follow-through, let the racket come around your waist. Watch to see where your opponent is going to hit the return.

Bend at the waist.

Drag your back foot forwards.

Bring this leg around to help you recover for your next shot.

The service return

AFTER THE SERVE, the service return is the most important shot. Not only do you have to keep the ball in court, but you also have to make it difficult for your opponent to play their next shot. The moment the server throws the ball up you will get an idea of the shot he or she has planned. If you are receiving a fast serve, stand about 1 m (3 ft) behind the baseline (it is easier to run forwards than backwards). If the serve is slower then move forwards into the court and aim to hit the ball at the top of the bounce. Try using your basic groundstrokes, then adapt them in ways that add power, direction, and consistency to the stroke. Remember, the server's aim is to win the point straight away. You must react quickly and try to stop them.

Take a guess
If you know your opponent well you may be able to predict how they will serve.

Ready position
Stand 1 m (3 ft) behind where you imagine you will be hitting the ball. As soon as the server throws the ball up, move forwards into a split-step (see page 38). This will help you to stay on your toes and will force your weight forwards so that you are ready to move quickly.

If your opponent's first serve is a fault, try standing just inside the baseline to show that you are ready to attack.

Double-handed backhand return
A double-handed backhand will give you extra strength to return a fast serve. Try to keep your racket between waist and shoulder height and lean into the ball. If your opponent knows that you have a strong double-handed backhand, it is very unlikely that they will serve the ball straight to your favourite stroke. If they serve wide, you may need to use a single-handed backhand to reach farther.

The take-back
The speed of your opponent's serve will determine how much time you have for your take-back. A soft serve gives you time to take your racket back fully and add more power to your shot, whereas a fast serve will require a short take-back. Whichever you use, make sure that you follow through properly.

On a long take-back bring your racket right back.

Turn your body sideways-on to the court.

Stand with your feet apart and your knees bent to help keep your balance.

If you only have time for a short take-back, use your weight to put extra power behind the shot.

Keep your wrists firm.

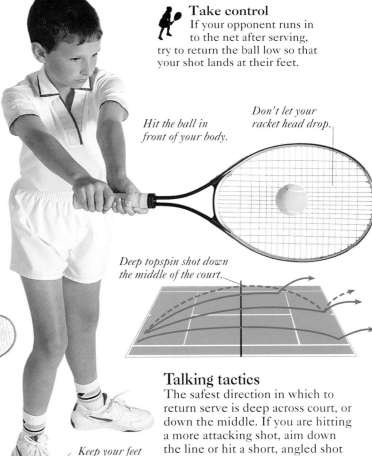

Take control
If your opponent runs in to the net after serving, try to return the ball low so that your shot lands at their feet.

Hit the ball in front of your body.

Don't let your racket head drop.

Deep topspin shot down the middle of the court.

Keep your feet shoulder-width apart.

Talking tactics
The safest direction in which to return serve is deep across court, or down the middle. If you are hitting a more attacking shot, aim down the line or hit a short, angled shot cross court.

High-driven forehand return

With this stroke you are counter-attacking the ball, sending it back to the server with equal or greater speed. From the ready position, take your racket back and quickly turn sideways-on to the court. If you are playing a forehand shot, rotate your shoulders and bring your weight onto your front foot as you drive your racket through. Keep your balance after the shot by bringing your racket leg forwards, then recover to the baseline for your next shot.

Keep your head still.

Your racket should be between waist and shoulder height.

Your racket travels over your opposite shoulder as you follow through.

Hit the ball in front of your body.

Semi-western forehand grip

Use your free arm for balance.

Topspin tip
Use topspin on your high-driven return to keep your opponent in a defensive position on their baseline.

Step forwards as you make your stroke.

Keep watching the ball.

To open the angle of your racket face, tilt it backwards.

Low-driven backhand return

To return a low bouncing ball on your backhand side, bend your knees and keep your body low as you step into the shot. Hit the ball in front of your body, with your racket head at a slightly open angle. This will lift the ball over the net.

Eastern backhand grip

Blocked forehand return

This is a very effective shot against a fast server. With a firm grip on your racket, use a short take-back and a volley-like punching action (see pages 26-27). Even though you may feel you are doing little to hit the ball, the speed of your opponent's serve and the correct angle of your racket face will combine to produce a deep return.

Slice it
Try using slice on the low backhand to give the shot lift and depth.

Aim to hit the ball on your racket's sweet spot.

Keep your wrist firm.

Chipped backhand return

To chip your return of serve, you need to use a short take-back and lean into the ball. Here, Steffi Graf of Germany shows the similarity between the chipped backhand return and the backhand volley. Notice how Graf turns her shoulders, taking the ball more to the side of her while keeping her racket arm straight. If the server runs in to the net, a chipped return will keep the ball low as it travels over the net and will make it land at the server's feet.

Step forwards into the ball.

25

Forehand volley

A VOLLEY IS A SHOT played when the ball is in its first flight, before it bounces. Stand in an attacking position about 2 m (6 ft) away from the net. Your volley action should be a short, sharp punch that has very little take-back or follow-through. Concentrate on the angle of the racket face so that the ball goes in the right direction. To begin with, use any forehand grip as this will give extra support to your wrist. When you become stronger, try to use a modified continental grip for your volleys.

Drive volley

If your opponent consistently hits the ball high and deep but without any pace, then surprise them occasionally by adapting your groundstroke into a volley. The drive volley requires practice as your take-back must be speedy. Try to return the ball before it bounces to disrupt your opponent's rhythm.

Use your free arm for balance.

Keep your head still and rotate your shoulders.

Move your weight from your back foot to your front foot.

1 Move forwards, turn your shoulders sideways, and take your racket back.

2 Move your weight forwards as you hit the ball in front of your body.

Double pressure
Playing doubles is a good way of improving your volleying because you are forced to move forwards more often.

Modified continental grip

Keep your knees bent.

Keep your feet shoulder-width apart and stay on your toes.

Start to turn your shoulders.

Your weight should be on this leg.

Watch the ball.

Keep a low centre of gravity as you step forwards.

Step forwards and move your weight onto your front foot.

Practising your volley

1 Stand in a ready position at the centre line. Your position near the net means there is less distance between you and your opponent. Your reactions therefore have to be quicker than at any other time during a rally.

2 As you see the ball coming towards you, start to take your racket back. The racket head should be slightly above the height at which you will hit the ball. Use a short take-back (see page 24) and keep your wrist firm.

3 Turn your shoulders and step forwards so that your weight is on your front foot. Hold the racket head high so that it forms a "V" shape with your forearm. Keep the racket face open (tilted backwards) and punch the racket forwards.

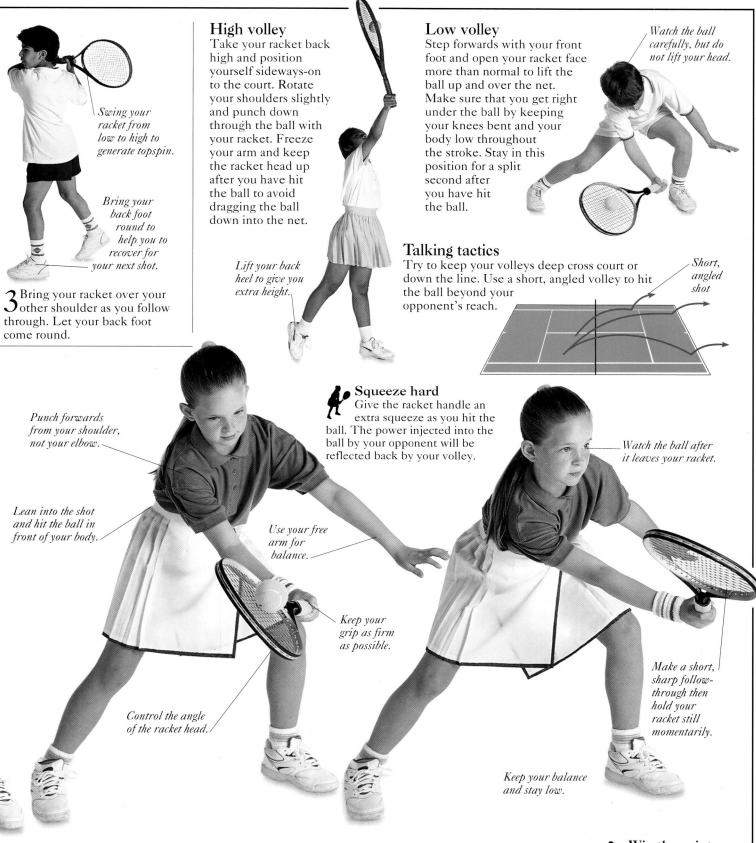

Swing your racket from low to high to generate topspin.

Bring your back foot round to help you to recover for your next shot.

3 Bring your racket over your other shoulder as you follow through. Let your back foot come round.

High volley

Take your racket back high and position yourself sideways-on to the court. Rotate your shoulders slightly and punch down through the ball with your racket. Freeze your arm and keep the racket head up after you have hit the ball to avoid dragging the ball down into the net.

Lift your back heel to give you extra height.

Low volley

Step forwards with your front foot and open your racket face more than normal to lift the ball up and over the net. Make sure that you get right under the ball by keeping your knees bent and your body low throughout the stroke. Stay in this position for a split second after you have hit the ball.

Watch the ball carefully, but do not lift your head.

Talking tactics

Try to keep your volleys deep cross court or down the line. Use a short, angled volley to hit the ball beyond your opponent's reach.

Short, angled shot

Squeeze hard
Give the racket handle an extra squeeze as you hit the ball. The power injected into the ball by your opponent will be reflected back by your volley.

Punch forwards from your shoulder, not your elbow.

Lean into the shot and hit the ball in front of your body.

Use your free arm for balance.

Keep your grip as firm as possible.

Control the angle of the racket head.

Watch the ball after it leaves your racket.

Make a short, sharp follow-through then hold your racket still momentarily.

Keep your balance and stay low.

4 Move forwards to meet the ball in front of your body. Guide the bottom edge of your racket in a slight downward path behind the back of the ball. This will put slice on the ball, helping you to aim your shot deep into your opponent's court.

5 The punching action of your shot will make the racket follow through slightly. As soon as this happens, freeze the racket face in the angle and the direction that you have hit the ball. This will help you to control the flight of the ball.

Win the point
Do not stay too close to the net after your volley or your opponent may hit a lob (see pages 30-31) to the back of your court.

Backhand volley

MANY PLAYERS FIND the backhand
volley easier to play than the forehand.
Exactly the same principles apply for both
shots, but the backhand volley often feels
more natural because it is played from a
sideways-on position. As well as an attacking
stroke, the backhand volley can be used as a
defensive shot if the ball is directed straight
at your body. You must be decisive and have
quick reflexes to reach the ball in a split
second. Try to use a continental grip, but if
your wrist is weak, change to a backhand
grip or use a double-handed grip.

High backhand volley

For this stroke you will need to have a strong wrist and a
firm grip to control the racket head. Don't let your racket
drop or shake when it hits the ball.

Use your free arm for balance.

Support the racket head with your free hand.

Turn your shoulders.

Hit the ball in front of your body.

Bend your knees ready to stretch up to the high ball.

1 When you see a high ball
approaching, turn sideways-
on to the court and take your
racket back high.

2 Punch through the ball with
your racket. Do not reach
over the net as you hit the ball
or you will lose the point.

Low backhand volley

A low volley is very difficult to turn into an attacking stroke
because it is below net height. As long as you get your body
down underneath the ball your shot need not be a defensive one.

1 As soon as you see that the
ball is low, turn your upper
body sideways-on to the court.
Bend your knees as you take
your racket back, supporting
the throat of the racket with your
free hand.

Keep your eyes on the ball.

Start to turn sideways.

Hold your racket head above wrist height.

Keep your head and body low to help you get your racket underneath the ball.

Your weight should be on your back foot ready to step forwards.

Move to meet the ball

When you play a volley, it is
essential to turn your shoulders
and take the ball in front of
your body. Yevgeny Kafelnikov
of Russia demonstrates this
well on his backhand side, as he
steps forwards to meet the ball.
Notice how he keeps the racket
head above his wrist.

2 Step forwards on your racket
side. Punch your racket head
under and up through the ball.
Open the racket head slightly
more than usual to give the
shot extra lift over
the net.

Lead with the bottom edge of your racket to add slice.

28

Try not to take your eyes off the ball as your arm moves across your view.

Stay sideways-on to the court with your racket arm outstretched.

3 Use a short follow-through and hold the racket head high and slightly open.

Double-handed drive volley with topspin

Try using a double-handed backhand drive action to volley a high, slow ball. This sometimes feels like swinging a baseball bat, but your wrists must stay firm. With a controlled take-back, move forwards and swing through the ball. To generate topspin on the ball, swing your racket up from low to high. Adding spin will control and guide the ball into court. If you prefer to hit on your forehand, you may have time on some shots to run around the backhand and play a forehand shot.

Keep your head still.

Hit the ball in front of your body.

Follow through with the racket over your other shoulder.

Attacking backhand volley

If the ball is at or above net level, try playing a more attacking backhand volley. From the ready position, take your racket back slightly. Step forwards on your racket foot and strike the ball with a firm punching action. Aim to hit the ball just over the top of the net and deep into your opponent's court. Keep the racket head above your wrist and follow through slightly. Briefly hold the racket head still before recovering.

Watch the ball leave your opponent's racket.

Make sure the action is from your racket shoulder and not your elbow.

Keep your head still and don't take your eyes off the ball.

Step forwards.

Turn your upper body sideways-on to the court.

Hit down through the back of the ball to generate slice.

Keep your racket head still for a moment.

3 Freeze your racket head as you hit the ball. Keep your body low for a split second, then return to the ready position for your next shot. Keep watching the ball all the time.

Stay compact and low.

Keep your knees bent or the ball will go into the net.

Your weight should be on your front foot.

On the rebound
When volleying off a fast ball, imagine your racket is a wall and let the ball simply rebound from it.

Use your free arm for balance.

Deep attacking shot

Talking tactics
An effective low volley can win the point. Try taking speed off the ball by loosening your grip on the racket slightly, and playing a short, angled shot. If your shot rises too high over the net, your opponent will have a chance to hit the ball past you.

The lob

A LOB SHOULD PASS HIGH over the top of your opponent's racket, otherwise they may take the opportunity to smash the ball back over the net. The flight of the ball must also be low enough so that your opponent doesn't have time to recover the shot. A high, deep lob is extremely useful in a variety of situations. It is most often used as a defensive shot, or instead of a groundstroke to counter-attack when your opponent has approached the net and played a volley.

Deep cross court shot with topspin

Talking tactics

Aim your lob deep over your opponent's backhand side. Hit cross court if the extra distance will help you to control the shot. The flight of the ball should be at its highest as it passes over your opponent's head. Remember that the wind will affect the flight of a high lob.

Flat backhand lob

If your opponent forces you out wide, or drives you back with a deep volley, then you are in a defensive position. Hit up a lob and force your opponent back to play the ball on their backhand side.

Watch the ball approaching.

Keep your head still.

Your follow-through is high with your racket out in front.

Use your free arm for balance.

Straighten up your body.

Continental grip

Bend your knees.

1 Take your racket back early and support it with your free hand.

2 Keep the racket face open as you bring your racket underneath the ball.

3 Swing the racket upwards through the ball. Push up with your knees to give the shot extra lift.

2 As the ball starts to fall, step into it, rotate your shoulders, and swing the racket forwards in a steep upwards path. Make sure the racket face is open to help the ball rise over your opponent's head. Hit the ball in front of your body and continue bringing your racket through in a smooth, rising action.

Take your racket back early.

Low forehand lob

Your opponent does not have to be at the net in order for you to lob. If you are driven out wide by an attacking shot, use a lob to give yourself time to prepare for your next shot. If your opponent has hit a smash over the net, use a lob with a short take-back. However, if you fail to put enough strength into your lob, the ball could fall short and give your opponent the chance to smash a winner.

1 Take an early back swing and turn your shoulders. Use either an eastern forehand grip or a continental grip so that you can hit underneath the ball effectively. If the ball is low, move forwards and bend your knees so that your preparation is low.

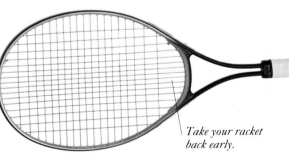

Keep your feet shoulder-width apart to help you balance.

Take control
If your lob is successful, try to take an attacking position at the net and win the point with an attacking volley or a smash.

3 Straighten your legs as the racket continues upwards. Use your other arm for balance. The stroke finishes with a high follow-through. The better your follow-through, the less likely it is that your lob will be short. After playing a lob, make sure you recover to a good position.

Keep your racket face open.

Keep your head still.

Your racket should make contact with the ball out in front of your body.

Rotate your shoulders.

Straighten your legs as you follow through with your racket.

Careful aim
Here, Michael Chang of America has run fast and kept low to get his racket underneath the ball and lift it up over his opponent's head. Chang's lob is high and deep enough to give him time to get in a strong attacking position for his next shot.

Fool your opponent
Try to disguise your lob by preparing it with a groundstroke back swing.

Double-handed backhand lob with topspin

If played successfully, this type of shot can win the point outright. An attacking lob is best played with topspin. This will make the ball loop over your opponent's head, drop rapidly, and kick up and away from your opponent.

Make your follow-through long and high.

Keep watching the ball.

1 Use either double-handed grip. Turn your shoulders and take your racket back early, as if you are preparing to hit a groundstroke.

2 Lower your racket with a looping action, and brush up behind the back of the ball from low to high. Keep the racket face open slightly.

3 Rotate your shoulders and straighten your body, pushing up with your knees. Follow through with the racket over your other shoulder.

The smash

THIS CAN BE THE MOST powerful tennis stroke, but it requires extra confidence and concentration to hit successfully. A smash is best played at the net to return a short lob, or off a high, weak ball after it has bounced. Use a similar action to that of your service stroke. Take care not to try to put too much power into the shot, but concentrate on your aim and timing. Place the ball deep, and to your opponent's weaker side. Your opponent has very little chance of returning a smash and, with practice, your smash could win the point outright.

Airborne attack

In order to reach a high lob, Pete Sampras of America leaps in the air to reach the ball before it passes over his head. At the same time, Sampras produces a winning smash that is aggressive and controlled. The camera has caught the snapping action of his wrist as the racket head travels over the ball. Athletic Sampras doesn't take his eyes off the ball even when his feet are 1 m (3 ft) off the ground!

Practising your jump smash

A jumping smash will enable you to reach a ball that you could not otherwise return. This stroke needs fine co-ordination in order to move into position and hit the ball while you are in midair. Make sure you prepare quickly, and move sideways-on to a position where you can "snap" your wrist over the ball and direct your shot down into your opponent's court.

Preparing to smash

Use the same throwing action with your racket arm as you do when serving (see pages 22-23). Point at the approaching ball with your free arm for balance and to help you guide your stroke.

Look up along your free arm at the ball.

Keep your racket shoulder lower than your ball shoulder to ensure a good throwing action.

Use your cross-over steps (see page 15) to move across the court.

Lead with the butt of the racket handle.

Start to bring your racket back.

Take the racket behind your shoulders, keeping your elbow high.

1 Turn sideways-on to the court. Bend your elbow as you start to lift your racket up. Point to the ball with your other hand and follow it as you move into position.

2 If the lob is deep, start to move back by crossing your front leg over your back leg.

3 Take a large final step with your back foot and bend your knees ready to jump. Move quickly but don't rush into your jump.

Jump up with your racket leg.

Angled smash

If you can't get enough power into your smash to hit the ball past your opponent, use an angled smash. Move towards the ball and get into the ready position quickly. Stretch your body and reach up to the ball. Imagine you are playing a second serve with spin, and use the bottom edge of the racket to brush around the ball and send it back with slice. Follow through with your racket around your waist.

Cut around the ball with the bottom edge of the racket.

Catch your body weight by bringing your back foot forwards.

Stand in a sideways-on position.

Backhand smash

If properly timed, it is possible to hit this shot with power. Always try to place your backhand smash deep to your opponent's weaker side, never straight down the middle of the court.

Support the racket head with your free hand.

Stand sideways-on to the court.

Run around

If the ball is coming to your backhand side, try and run around it to hit a more powerful smash on your forehand side.

Reach up to the ball with the contact point out in front of your body.

Follow through with the racket low in front of you.

4 As you begin to "throw" your racket upwards, turn your shoulders into the shot. Push with your back leg to jump up to the ball.

Keep your head still as you turn your shoulders.

5 With your shoulders turned, reach up to the ball and bring the racket head over your wrist very quickly to produce a "snapping" effect. The contact point should be in front of your body.

Hit the ball with the sweet spot on your racket strings.

Talking tactics

From your position at the net, hit a powerful smash down into the court so the ball bounces over your opponent's head, or deep to your opponent's weaker side. Try sending an angled smash out wide occasionally.

7 As you land, catch the momentum of your weight by bringing your racket foot forwards.

Bring the racket head down through the ball.

6 Bring your racket down as you hit the ball. Let your free arm come around to slow down the twist in your upper body.

Stretch your whole body as you reach to hit the ball ahead of you.

Guide the ball

Take care not to drag the ball down into the net.

Follow through with your racket around your waist.

Bring your back foot forwards to help you keep your balance.

The drop shot

A WINNING GAME is not just about hitting as many powerful shots as possible. It is also about moving your opponent around, making spaces on the court into which you can attack. The drop shot will improve your ability to explore the size of the court. The drop shot is an example of a "touch" shot used to catch out an overly defensive baseline player. It will force your opponent up to the net where you can then hit a passing drive, or a lob. Taking the pace off the ball and directing it with an accurate drop shot is typical of a "touch" game. This is a soft stroke that will not necessarily win you the point straight away, but will move your opponent out of position.

Backhand drop shot

Some players find it easier to play a drop shot on their backhand side. The backhand slicing action can feel more natural because of the side-on position. If you normally use a two-handed backhand, try to play with one hand for this soft stroke.

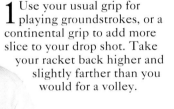

Rotate your shoulders.

Keep your racket face open. This will lift the ball just over the net.

Move your weight onto your front foot.

1 Use a high take-back, and hold the racket with the grip you normally use for backhand slice.

2 Cut down behind the ball with the edge of your racket then up through the hitting area.

Forehand drop shot

Try playing a drop shot from a short mid-court ball after you have pushed your opponent back with several deep shots. If you do not play an effective drop shot, then move back into a defensive position. If you play it well, move slightly forwards so you can reach a counter drop shot from your opponent.

1 Use your usual grip for playing groundstrokes, or a continental grip to add more slice to your drop shot. Take your racket back higher and slightly farther than you would for a volley.

Turn sideways-on to the court and follow the ball carefully with your free arm.

Start to turn your shoulders.

2 With a relaxed grip, start to bring your racket forwards, leading with the bottom edge of the racket. There should be a slight downward path to your swing.

Keep your knees bent.

Step forwards with your weight on your front foot.

Talking tactics

Try not to play a drop shot from too far back on court as the ball is less likely to clear the net. Wait for a shorter mid-court ball. Hit the ball softly with slice into an open space away from your opponent. The ball should already be dropping as it crosses the net and then will bounce very little.

Keep your head still and your free shoulder back.

3 Follow through slightly up beyond the point of contact, with the racket facing in the direction you have hit the ball.

Disguised drop shot

An excellent way of catching your opponent off guard is to play a disguised drop shot. Take your racket back early as you would for a normal groundstroke, and look as if you intend to hit a drive. At the last minute, slow down the racket to play your drop shot.

Use a full take-back of the racket.

Cut underneath the ball at the last minute.

Step forwards to the ball.

Drop volley

1 While a drop shot is played as a ground-stroke after the bounce, a drop volley is played at the net before the bounce. Prepare as you would to play a normal volley, stepping forwards with a short take-back, and hitting the ball in front of your body.

2 Keep a very relaxed grip and as the ball hits your racket strings, allow the racket head to move back and absorb the force of the shot. This deadens the speed of the ball and allows you to just clear the net with your shot.

Practice makes perfect
While practising your drop shot, see how many bounces it takes for the ball to travel to your opponent's service line. More than three and it is a good, soft drop shot.

Keep your head still.

Keep the racket head above your wrist.

Your shoulders are turned and facing the net.

Lean into the ball.

Use your other arm to help keep you steady.

3 As the ball approaches your racket, open the racket face. Cut up and through the ball with the bottom edge of your racket and send the ball back with slice. Keep your grip relaxed to take the pace off the ball.

Contact point is in front of your body.

4 Let your racket follow through to gently lift the ball over the net. Use only a short follow-through and keep the racket facing in the direction you have hit the ball.

35

Playing at the baseline

A LL TENNIS PLAYERS, from beginners to more advanced players, use the five fundamental skills (see page 17). These are especially important when rallying with an opponent from the back of the court. The standard at which you play at the baseline depends on your ability and tactical awareness. As this improves, you should become familiar with the kind of decisions you need to make: where to move to in order to play a good shot, and how or when to make your stroke. At first your decisions will be conscious ones, but with more practice, you will start to make decisions automatically, without actually thinking about them.

Stand in the ready position on the T of the service line and keep your eyes on the ball as it leaves your partner's racket.

Step with your racket leg for a backhand shot.

Level two

When you start rallying from the baseline, you will notice how much ground you have to cover (see below). You will move farther and will receive a greater variety of shots at the baseline than from farther forwards in court. This leads you to the next major decision: where to move to. Movement from side to side is linked to the first level and depends on whether the shot is forehand or backhand. Now you also have to move forwards if the ball lands short, or backwards if the ball is travelling high and deep.

Level one

To get an idea of what baseline play is like, begin by rallying with your opponent from service line to service line. At this stage, the first major decision is whether your shot will be forehand or backhand (see above). The quicker you can decide, the quicker you can react to the approaching ball. After hitting the ball, recover to your home base (see page 38) at the "T" of the service line.

Be ready
Concentrate on the ball so that you can anticipate how high and fast it is travelling over the net towards you.

As you move forwards to a short ball, turn sideways-on and take your racket back early.

After each shot, try to recover to your home base position on the baseline (see page 38). From here, watch your opponent return the ball.

Move back quickly for a high ball to allow it to drop to a comfortable height before hitting it.

Quickly move sideways to a wide ball with your racket ready.

For forehand shots, step across with your opposite leg. Make sure you keep a comfortable distance between the ball and your body.

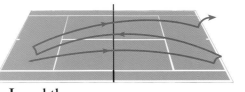

Level three

Once you feel comfortable moving to the ball and hitting it anywhere in court, you can begin to decide how you are going to play the shot. Start by trying to direct the ball diagonally across the court or down the sideline. Vary the height at which you hit the ball over the net and experiment with your spins. Also try changing the direction of the ball. Hitting from down the line to cross court is easier than changing from cross court to down the line, because you are less likely to hit the ball out.

Level four

By this stage, you should be considering what you intend to do with the shot. Three options apply to every shot: to rally, attack, or defend. These choices relate to your position on court. From the

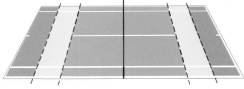

defensive rally zone (red), you should hit deep rally shots consistently into your opponent's rally zone. Defensive shots are also played when you are scrambling the ball back into play. From the setting up zone (yellow), you can start to hit harder rally shots and sometimes go for a deep or angled attacking shot. From the attacking zone (green), you attack the ball with both groundstrokes and volleys, and when you have the opening, hit a winner!

1 If you are drawn to one side with a high deep ball, take a short back swing and try to hit the ball as it rises.

Move without stepping back from the baseline.

Level five

At this stage, you should aim to hit the ball early, when it is rising or at the top of the bounce, brake after the shot (see below), and use a different type of recovery, called "centre point" recovery. The centre point is halfway between the two extreme possibilities of your opponent's return. For example, if you send a rally shot deep cross court, the centre point would be on the near side of the small T on the baseline. The ball is more likely to come back cross court, but you must be prepared to cover the other area of the court.

Centre point

Contact point should be around chest height, in front of your body.

2 When rallying at the baseline you should try to hit more cross court shots. After playing the stroke, brake your movement by bringing your back foot across.

Step into the shot.

3 With your braking foot, push yourself back into court and recover to a centre point position, just to one side of the small T on the baseline. From there you should be ready to reach anywhere on court to return the next shot.

Braking foot

Playing at the net

WHEN YOU START PLAYING tennis, you will hit groundstrokes from the baseline most of the time. You may move forwards to return a short ball when necessary before recovering back to the baseline. There is another option, however, and that is to move closer to the net to play volleys. The two strongest positions on court are "home base" position behind the centre of the baseline, and "home base" position 2 m (6 ft) back from the middle of the net. Your home bases are linked by two types of attacking shot: the approach shot (see below) and the serve.

Serve and volley

This tactic (right) is often used to pressurize the opponent's return of serve, and is most effective when playing doubles, or singles on a fast surface like grass.

1 Throw the ball up in front of you so your body weight is moving forwards.

2 As you move forwards after the serve, look up to see how your opponent is going to play their return.

3 Split-step as your opponent returns the ball.

Approach and volley

An approach shot is played from a ball that has landed short, making you move forwards to reach it. Use your approach shot to put your opponent under pressure. Hit the ball deep to your opponent's weaker side, using topspin to make the ball bounce away from them, or slice to keep the ball low. The lower and deeper you keep your approach shots, the more chance you will have of an easy return that you can put away. Alternatively, if you hit the ball down the middle of the court, you will limit the angle your opponent can use to hit an attacking return.

Practising your split-step

Use a split-step as your opponent plays their shot. It will help to equalize your balance and will prepare you to spring to one side for your volley. After recovering to either home base position, perform a split-step before playing your next shot. Simply plant your feet parallel to each other, shoulder-width apart, and bend your knees.

Let your body weight carry you forwards through the shot and towards the net.

1 You must be prepared at all times to move forwards for a short ball, as this will be an ideal chance to attack your opponent from the net position. Stay on your toes in the ready position. Watch the ball as it leaves your opponent's racket and quickly decide on your next move.

2 If the ball is short, move forwards to take it early when it is at the top of the bounce. The quicker you play the shot, the less time your opponent will have to recover and prepare for their next shot. However, it is important not to rush the stroke or get too close to the ball.

3 Move forwards, bringing your body weight through the approach shot. As you see your opponent hit the ball back, perform a split-step. How close you get to the net will depend on how fast the ball is travelling towards you. Try to move inside the service line.

4 Step forwards to meet the volley in front of your body.

5 Move in again to home base position and split-step for your next volley.

6 When you are in home base at the net, keep your body low and your knees bent, and do not move forwards again. Hit an attacking volley if your opponent's shot is high, or place the volley when the ball is below net height. You can also play a drop volley from here (see page 35).

Forehand step

When you volley, it is important that your contact point with the ball is in front of your body. To help play a volley correctly, step forwards to meet the ball rather than waiting for it to come to you. After split-stepping, keep your knees bent and your weight moving forwards in a continuous motion. Step forwards with your racket foot for a backhand shot, and your other foot for a forehand shot. To reach for a wider ball, step farther across the court.

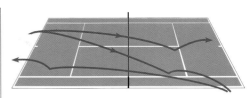

Talking tactics

When you serve and volley, be aware that a wide serve will give your opponent more angle to use for a passing return. Aim down the middle of the service box most of the time, and only occasionally serve out wide to your opponent's weaker side.

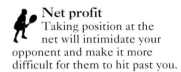

Net profit
Taking position at the net will intimidate your opponent and make it more difficult for them to hit past you.

Talking tactics

When you hit a wide approach shot or volley, position yourself off-centre to the side that you have hit the ball. This will enable you to cover a down-the-line passing shot. When you are at the net you can already intercept the cross court shot.

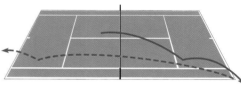

Attack or defend?
Successful net play is a combination of knowing when to attack or defend. In both cases, keep your volley action short and sharp.

Hold your racket up ready to move to a forehand or backhand shot.

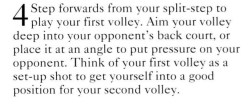

4 Step forwards from your split-step to play your first volley. Aim your volley deep into your opponent's back court, or place it at an angle to put pressure on your opponent. Think of your first volley as a set-up shot to get yourself into a good position for your second volley.

5 If you are not in a good home base position after hitting your first volley, move forwards again and perform a split-step. It is important not to get too close to the net or you may touch it with your racket, or your opponent can easily lob the ball over your head.

6 Step forwards from your split-step for your second volley. If your earlier shots went well, it is likely that you can use this shot to win the point. If the ball is high, attack the volley without swinging your racket. If the ball is below net height, think more carefully where to place the ball.

Doubles

P LAYING DOUBLES is all about team work. You and your partner should understand each other's strengths and weaknesses so that you can play well together. The doubles court includes the tramline area so there is a larger court area in which to aim, but a smaller court area for each player to cover. When you first start to play doubles, you may feel safer staying back on the baseline and hitting groundstrokes. Once you feel more confident as a doubles pair, try to play volleys from an attacking position at the net as much as possible.

Doubles service rules

If you and your partner have won first serve, tactically it is best for the stronger server to serve for the first game. If you serve first, your partner will be the third person to serve. All four players take it in turns to serve; your opponents serve second and fourth. Players also take turns to receive the service. The scoring and rules are the same as in the singles game (see pages 12-13 and 44).

Covering the court

If you and your partner both cover the middle of the court, your opponents will be forced to aim their shots wide. This increases their chances of hitting the ball out of court.

When serving, try to serve deep so you have more time to prepare for your next shot.

Your partner must try not to let a gap open up or leave any part of the court out of reach.

Serving

If you and your partner are serving, you automatically have the advantage of being able to claim the net position first by serving and volleying. As you serve, your partner should be in an attacking position close to the net. From there, he or she should be able to reach a down-the-middle or down-the-tramline ball, depending on how the return of service is played. When serving, stand at the baseline, farther towards the tramlines than when playing singles, in order to cover a possible angled return. At the beginning of each new point, swap sides with your partner.

Return of serve

With two people on the other side of the net, it is more important to return accurately rather than powerfully. If, after serving, your opponent comes straight in to a net position, then aim the ball at their feet as he or she is moving forwards. Alternatively, make them stretch for a short, angled shot. If the server stays back, then return the ball deep to the baseline and claim the net position yourself. At the start of each new point, the player who was receiving at the baseline for the previous point moves forwards, and their partner moves back ready to return the next serve.

Move forwards to meet the ball.

Your partner stands on the service line ready to move in to volley.

A problem shared

Here, Martina Navratilova of America has managed to jump up with enough height to reach a lob. However, notice her partner, Jon Stark. Throughout the shot he is ready to move back to retrieve the ball just in case Martina doesn't reach it. If Martina had missed her lob, she would have moved to the left court to cover Stark's side. Good doubles partners must be prepared to cover for each other like this.

On the court

When serving and receiving, it is normal for each pair to have one player at the baseline and one near the net. Generally the server and receiver play the point out between them. Both baseline players rally until they get a chance to move forwards, and join their partners in an attacking position at the net. Meanwhile, the net players are covering their own side of the court, waiting for an opportunity to intercept the ball.

Your partner should keep an equal distance away from you – as if attached by a piece of string.

Decision making
Discuss tactics before and during the game. Try to make sure that your partner always knows your next move.

Volleying

If you and your partner are both at the net, keep an equal distance apart. Move sideways, backwards, and forwards together. As you retrieve the ball, your partner must stop any large spaces from opening up. Your opponents may try to hit attacking shots down the middle of the court in order to confuse you, so it is best if you decide before the match which one of you will cover this type of shot. When you are both positioned at the net, there is a chance that you will be lobbed. Call to your partner to decide who will return each ball.

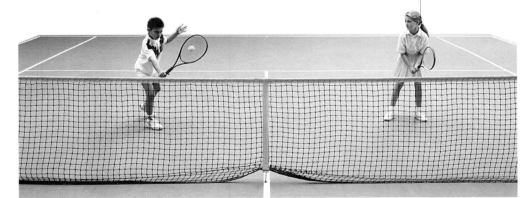

Intercepting the ball

At any time during a rally, the players positioned at the net should be ready to intercept. This is a quick and easy way to win a point from a high, slow groundstroke. Even if your interception doesn't win the point, it is a good opportunity to attack. Start to move across to your partner's side of the court once your opponent has begun to take their shot. Do not move across too early or your opponent may change their plans and hit the ball past you down the tramline. Your partner at the baseline should cover the side that you have just left.

You should try to move across and intercept any shot that is within reach.

Your partner moves over to cover the side that you have just left and stays there.

Coaching and tournaments

TENNIS IS A GAME of wits as well as an athletic challenge. Once you have started classes, your mental game should begin to improve along with your technique. You may enjoy taking part in competitions arranged by your school or club. As you progress, you will compete against more experienced players and you will need commitment and determination in order to succeed. Very few players reach world class level, and even the best players always hope to improve their game. But whether you play or just spectate, tennis is one of the most popular and dramatic sports in the world.

Wheelchair tennis
The International Wheelchair Tennis Federation (IWTF) rules are basically the same as regular tennis rules. Players have specially designed sports wheelchairs that are easy to manoeuvre around the court. The ball is allowed to bounce twice – the second bounce can land outside the court boundaries.

Classes and coaching
Group lessons are good fun for beginners. However, one-to-one coaching will give you a greater understanding of your own abilities and can help you to concentrate and develop your own technique. Find a coach who is enthusiastic, knowledgeable and supportive. A good coach should be capable of teaching tennis to people of all abilities. Ask at your school or local tennis club for information. Alternatively, contact one of the professional associations listed on page 45.

International competition
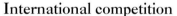
Playing professional tennis requires absolute dedication, long hours of travelling, and intense training. At tournaments such as the Monte Carlo Open in France (above) temperatures can soar and players must learn not to let the weather affect their game.

Keeping watch
The International Tennis Federation (ITF) is the overall governing body of the game worldwide. Most countries have their own tennis associations to ensure standard rules are kept and to organize national leagues and tournaments. Some events are so huge that many matches are played simultaneously. Grounds need to be vast to accommodate the games and crowds, like the one above at Wimbledon, London, which has 14 courts.

World ranking
Professional players are ranked or "seeded" by their number of wins. The more wins, the better the seed. Boris Becker of Germany (above) is currently the world men's Number Three seed. Ranking guarantees that the better players remain in the final stages of the tournaments.

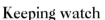

Major international tournaments

The Grand Slam
This consists of four annual International Open Championships:
The Australian Open in January
The French Open in May/June
The British Open (Wimbledon) in June/July
The US Open in August/September
At each of these four tournaments there is a men's singles winner, a women's singles winner, men's doubles, women's doubles and mixed doubles winners, as well as junior winners.

The Davis Cup
Four groups made up of over 100 nations compete for this trophy throughout each year.

The Federation Cup
The premier team competition in women's tennis. From April to November every year, over 80 nations battle for promotion within the three groups in the Fed Cup, as it is now known.

Glossary

During your tennis coaching, or when watching tennis, you may find it helpful to understand some of the following terms and phrases.

A

Ace A service which lands out of reach of the receiver.

Advantage The next point to be won after deuce; advantage server or advantage receiver.

Approach shot A groundstroke made when running towards the net in expectation of playing a volley.

B

Backcourt The area behind the baseline. Also called the run back.

Backspin See Slice.

Baseline game A method of play where the player remains at the back of the court.

Block A short, punched groundstroke used to return a fast travelling ball.

C

Cannonball service An extremely fast service of 161 kph (100 mph) or more.

Centre mark The 10.16 cm (4 in) line in the middle of the baseline at each end of the court. Also called the "small T".

Centre service line Divides the service area into two halves – left and right courts. Also called first and second courts.

Chip A short, sometimes angled, return; usually hit with slice.

Cross court A stroke played diagonally across the court.

D

Default A match is won by default if the opponent is absent or stops play before the match finishes.

Deuce The score whenever players are at 40-40, or have an even score after six points of a game.

Double fault Two successive serving faults, causing the server to lose the point.

Down-the-line A shot played parallel to the sidelines.

Drive A groundstroke played between waist and shoulder height, in which the ball is driven deep into the opponent's court.

Drop shot A ball hit lightly with underspin, which lands just over the other side of the net.

F

Fault A ball that fails to land in the correct court.

Fifteen all The score as each player has scored one point. The word "all" is used instead of "each".

First flight The flight of the ball after it has been struck and before it bounces.

Flat stroke A ball hit without spin.

Follow-through The continuation of the racket after the ball has been struck.

Forecourt The area between the service line and the net.

H

Half volley A stroke where the racket meets the ball at the moment the ball bounces.

L

Let A ball that touches the net after it is served, but still falls into the correct area of the opponent's court. The serve is taken again.

Love The tennis term for zero when scoring. Believed to have come from the french *l'oeuf*, meaning egg. It was joked that the zero looked like an egg on the scoreboard.

M

Match point The score when one player needs only one more point to win the match.

N

Net ball A ball that touches the net but remains in play and the rally continues. Also called net cord.

Net game Playing all your shots in an attacking position at the net in order to hurry your opponent and force them to make mistakes.

No man's land The area between the service line and the baseline.

P

Passing shot A shot which sends the ball beyond the reach of an opponent who is attacking from the net.

R

Rally A prolonged series of strokes played back from one player to another.

Retire When a player concedes victory before the completion of a match.

Retrieve To return a ball which is difficult to reach or handle.

Return The stroke that returns the service. Can also describe any shot during a rally.

S

Second flight The flight of the ball after it has bounced once.

Set There are six games in a set and three sets in a match (five sets for professional male players).

Set up An easy return from which the opponent can hit a winner.

Slice Also called sidespin or backspin. The ball is "sliced" with the racket to spin it sideways and backwards. The ball veers slightly in the direction of the spin in flight and more significantly after the bounce. Usually imparted during the service.

Stop volley A volley which absorbs the velocity of the ball and drops it just over the net.

T

Take-back The back swing in preparation for the stroke.

Tiebreak Comes into operation at six games all. The winner is the first to reach seven points (or the first to gain a two-point lead if the tiebreak score reaches six all). A tiebreak is not played in the final set, which must be won by two clear games.

Topspin A forward spin that makes the ball dip in flight and then bounce higher than normal. The top of the ball spins forwards in the direction of its flight. Achieved by stroking the racket up behind the back of the ball.

Touch game Tactical play using soft strokes at the net.

Tramlines The name given to the parallel lines running down both sides of the tennis court. The outer is the boundary of the doubles court, the inner is the boundary of the singles court.

More Tennis Rules

When to serve: The server must not serve until the receiver is ready. If the receiver attempts to return the service, they shall be deemed ready.

Player loses the point:
a. if, in playing the ball, they deliberately carry or catch it on their racket or deliberately touch it with their racket more than once.
b. if the player, their racket, clothing, or anything they are carrying touches the net, the posts, or their opponent's court while the ball is in play.
c. if the player volleys the ball before it has passed the net.
d. if the ball in play touches a player or anything that they are wearing or carrying, except their racket or hands.
e. if they throw their racket and it hits the ball.
f. if they deliberately and materially change the shape of their racket during the playing of the point.

Player hinders opponent: If a player deliberately commits any act which hinders their opponent in making a stroke, then they shall lose the point. If the act was involuntary, the point should be replayed.

Changing ends: When changing ends, a maximum of one minute 30 seconds shall pass from the moment the ball goes out of play at the end of one game to the time the first ball is struck for the next game.

Time between points: Must not exceed 25 seconds.

Coaching: A player must not receive coaching during a match unless in a team competition.

It is a good return if:
a. the ball is returned outside the posts, provided that it hits the ground within the proper court.
b. a player's racket passes over the net after they have returned the ball, provided the ball passes the net before being played and is properly returned.
c. a player succeeds in returning the ball in play, which has struck another ball lying in the court.

Order of serve: If a player serves out of turn, the player who should have served shall serve as soon as the mistake is discovered. All points scored before such a discovery still stand. If a game is completed before such a discovery, the order of service shall remain as altered.

Scoring: If there is a disagreement in scores, then both players shall return to the last agreed score.

Index

Useful addresses

These tennis organizations may be able to help you to find a local club or coach to give you guidance. Ask at your school as well – it may have its own teaching scheme.

The Lawn Tennis Association
The Queen's Club
West Kensington
London W14 9EG
Tel: (0171) 381 7000
Information Line: (0171) 381 7111

British Schools Lawn Tennis Association
c/o The Queen's Club
West Kensington
London W14 9EG
Tel: (0171) 381 7000

International Tennis Federation
Palliser Road
Barons Court
London W14 9EN
Tel: (0171) 381 8060

Tennis Ireland
Argyle Square
Donnybrook
Dublin 4
Tel: (00353) 1 6681841

National Wheelchair Tennis Association
Martin McElhatton
72 Woodmere
Barton Hills
Luton, Beds LU3 4ND
Tel: (01582) 570662

The Professional Tennis Coaches Association
The Queen's Club
West Kensington
London W14 9EG
Tel: (0171) 381 7000

The Scottish Lawn Tennis Association
12 Melville Crescent
Edinburgh EH3 7LU
Tel: (0131) 225 1284

The Welsh Lawn Tennis Association
Plymouth Chambers
3 Westgate Street
Cardiff CF1 1JF
Tel: (01222) 371 838

European Tennis Association
Seltisbergerstrasse 6
CH 4059 Basel
Switzerland
Tel: (41) 61 331 7675

Steven Vance   Jessica London   Vishal Nayyar   Faye Mason   Nick Hamnabard   Namita Shah   Nick Çava Day

Acknowledgments

Dorling Kindersley would like to thank the following people for their kind help in the production of this book:

Kester Jackson, tennis coach, who has been invaluable at every stage of this book's production; All the Young Tennis Players for their skill and enthusiasm during the photographic sessions, also to their families; The Parklangley Tennis and Squash Club, Beckenham, Kent, for their help, patience, and hospitality; The Lawn Tennis Association, Wimbledon, London, for providing useful information; Bromley Lawn Tennis and Squash Club, Bromley, Kent, for allowing us the use of their indoor court; Carole Orbell for help during photography sessions; Jason Page for his editorial advice; Chetan Joshi and Floyd Sayers for their design assistance.

Picture credits
Key: c=centre; b=bottom; r=right; l=left; t=top.

Russ Adams Productions Inc.: front cover, 8bc, 8br, 13bl, inside back cover;

Action Plus/Chris Barry: 12b, Mike Hewitt: 42cl; **Allsport UK Ltd.:** 28cr/ Clive Brunskill: 25bc, 32tr, Neale Haynes: 42t, Gray Mortimore: 42cr, Gary M. Prior: 13br, 23tl, 42bc, Chris Raphael: 12c; **Colorsport:** 41tr; **Robert Harding Picture Library**/ Adam Woolfitt: 42bl; **Hulton-Deutsch Collection:** 9tl, 9c, 9cr; **Carol L. Newsom:** 8tl, 9br, back cover; **Sporting Pictures (UK) Ltd.:** 9bl, 31tr; **Wimbledon Tennis Museum:** 9bc.

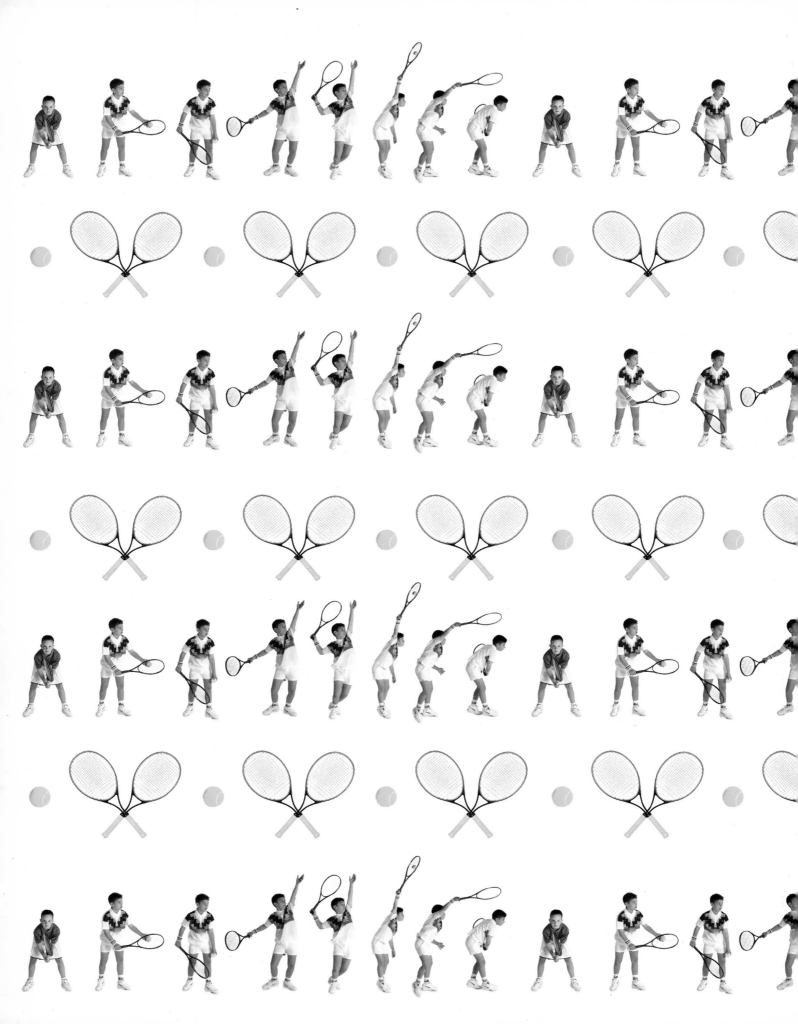